UNDERCOVER STORY

THE HIDDEN STORY OF
GANGS AND CRIME

Karen Latchana Kenney

rosen publishing's
rosen central

New York

Published in 2014 by The Rosen Publishing Group, Inc.
29 East 21st Street
New York, NY 10010

First Edition

Produced for Rosen by Calcium Creative Ltd.
Editor for Calcium Creative Ltd.: Sarah Eason and Ronne Randall
Designer: Keith Williams

Photo credits: Cover: Shutterstock: Jason Stitt. Inside: Dreamstime: Americanspirit 36, 39,
41, 43, Anitapatterson 23, Annieannie 13, Bdingman 10, Crystalcraig 26, Deanwthompson 6,
Dwphotos 35, Ejwhite 12, Enigmatico 44, Gatordawg 11, Jfeinstein 5, Julijah 14, Kevingrotz
34, Mitarart 29, Monkeybusinessimages 15, 33, Oriontrail 30, Phartisan 38, Philcold 19,
Reba 31, Sangiorzboy 25, Wlablack 8; Shutterstock: Africa Studio 28, AlexAranda 21, Sylvie
Bouchard 32, Djem 16, Dotshock 42, Maridav 17, Monkey Business Images 7, Nejron Photo
1, 4, Nomad_Sou 18, Rikke 22, StockPhotosLV 27, Straight 8 Photography 40, Villorejo 9,
Zagunov 24, Dmitry Zubarev 37.

Library of Congress Cataloging-in-Publication Data

Kenney, Karen Latchana.
The hidden story of gangs and crime/Karen Latchana Kenney.—First edition.
        pages cm.—(Undercover story)
Includes bibliographical references and index.
Audience: Grades 5 to 8.
ISBN 978-1-4777-2799-7 (library binding)
1. Gangs—United States—Juvenile literature. 2. Juvenile delinquency—United States—Juvenile
literature. I. Title.
HV6439.U5K46 2014
364.106'60973—dc23
                                                                                    2013022783

Manufactured in the United States of America

CPSIA Compliance Information: #W14YA: For further information, contact Rosen Publishing, New York, New York, at 1-800-237-9932.

CONTENTS

THE TRUTH ABOUT GANGS

Across the United States you will find gangs, and the numbers are growing. There are around 1.4 million gang members, and there are around 33,000 gangs. Many communities deal with the negative and deadly effects resulting from gang activities. Innocent people are shot in gang wars on the streets. Young people in gangs die every day. Neighborhood streets become unsafe to walk, and drugs and crime threaten the safety of community members.

WHAT ARE GANGS?

Gangs are large organized groups of people who have a common purpose. They may participate in criminal activities, such as drug dealing or gun violence. They may have a common color, sign or symbol, and name. Most gang members are male, but more and more female members are joining. Gangs are found in all social and ethnic groups, too. Many recruit members at a young age and have leaders that direct the gang's operations. Gangs usually also claim power over certain areas of communities.

Gangs attract teen recruits in all parts of the United States.

Gangs have been around for many years. They form in all kinds of communities, and can bring guns and crimes to the streets. For vulnerable teens they offer a kind of family, making them feel like they belong and are loved, and protecting them from other gangs in dangerous neighborhoods. Teens may feel that they have a purpose in a gang, especially in communities that lack opportunities and are run-down.

But this gang family can lead teens to crime and drug abuse. And in many cases, belonging to a gang means an early death.

This book examines the issue of gangs and the crime involved with them. It covers the reasons why teens join gangs and the ways they get out. Gangs are an ever-growing issue—one that threatens communities in many ways.

Some graffiti is made by gangs, marking their territories

CHAPTER ONE

ALL ABOUT GANGS

Frank K's gang was the Juntos Queridos Asesinos (JQA), a violent gang in Houston, Texas. The gang's name is Spanish for "Together Beloved Assassins." Frank joined the JQA when he was only 10 years old, and soon his younger brother also joined. Frank was inked with gang tattoos, and he dressed like a gang member.

Frank slowly moved up the ranks of the gang. When he was 19 he began recruiting new members. He made sure that all of the schools in the gang's territory were controlled by the JQA. His brother had similar gang duties.

Soon other gang members targeted Frank. In 2011, a rival gang assaulted him. They were paying back the JQA for the murder of one of their members. Then Frank's home was burglarized. The violence was hitting closer and closer to home.

Violence is part of a gang member's life.

BREAKING NEWS

>> According to the 2011 National Youth Gang Survey, two out of every five gang members are under the age of 18—about 35 percent of the total number. The age of members also depends on

INTO GANG LIFE

Like Frank, many new gang members are recruited at a young age. Many join as adolescents, between the ages of 14 and 16. This is a time when teens are changing and figuring out who they are. They may be lured in by the promise of money and power, and by the gang's loyalty among its members. Young recruits have an advantage, too. They cannot be tried as adults in legal courts for the crimes they commit, and they can quickly return to the gang after serving their time in juvenile detention centers. This makes young members valuable to a gang.

Young people are often recruited to be new gang members

where the gang is located. In rural areas and small cities, where gangs are newer, more members are younger. In large cities and suburban counties, where gangs have been around longer, there are more adult gang members.

Not all gangs are the same. They are very complex groups. Some operate on a national level, others are much smaller and can only be found in a certain local area. Gangs may only include members of one ethnic group, or only males or females, or they can be more diverse. There are three main types of criminal gangs:

Street Gangs: A street gang operates in a city, suburb, or rural area and is the type found in most parts of the United States. It forms on the street and each one controls a certain territory. Some street gangs are part of a larger national group. Other street gangs are local ones that can only be found in one area of a city.

Prison Gangs: This gang type forms inside jail systems across the United States. The members of a prison gang are prisoners, who operate from within a jail, where the criminal activity takes place.

Outlaw Motorcycle Gangs:
An outlaw motorcycle gang (OMG) is made up of motorcycle club members. They use their motorcycle club to conduct criminal activity. Some OMGs are called "One Percenters," which comes from a statement made in the 1960s that 99 percent of motorcyclists were law-abiding citizens. OMG members pledge to use violence and act in criminal ways.

This Italian mural shows an armed gang.

Among other gang types are hybrid gangs, hate groups, and occult groups. Hybrid gangs are local gangs with less structure than most street gangs. They may change their name suddenly or members might belong to several gangs at once. A hate group is a gang of people who have a shared hatred of another group. Their hatred may be against people of a certain race or sexuality. And an occult group may practice satanic worship or heavily use drugs. All of these gangs use violence in different ways.

Motorcycle gangs can quickly move drugs across the country.

UNDERCOVER STORY
THE BIGGEST GANGS

There are hundreds of groups operating in different states under the same main gang names. Some of these national gangs are very well known, including the Bloods and Crips, the Black Gangster Disciples, and the Latin Kings. The Latin Kings is the largest Hispanic gang in the United States. It has around 18,000 members and is found in 34 states. The Bloods and the Crips are two rival gangs that started in Los Angeles, California, in the 1950s. These gangs have since spread across the country. The Bloods are known by their red bandannas or clothing. Blue is the color of the Crips. The Black Gangster Disciples is an African-American gang. This gang is heavily involved with dealing drugs and is known to be very violent.

Street gangs can be found in almost every part of the United States—from rural areas to towns and cities—though the spread of the problem varies widely, depending on the kind of area. Approximately 41 percent of all US gangs are found in larger cities, and 31 percent are in smaller cities. Suburban counties are where just over 23 percent of the gangs are found, while rural counties contain the fewest gangs—less than 5 percent.

COMMUNITY ISSUES

There are certain factors in communities that can help gangs form. Gangs usually take root in areas that are socially disadvantaged and that have high crime rates. This means that there may be poverty, unemployment, and one-parent households, with many children in those homes. In these areas, there are often problems within families. There may also be poor school systems where many teens drop out.

With these factors, there is often not enough adult supervision. The one parent may have to work many hours to support the family. Or an older grandparent may be overwhelmed and unable to take care of the kids in a family. This means teens may have lots of free time without adults watching them.

Tags are often signs of gang activity.

There are also often few career or job opportunities. Teens who have dropped out of school lack education, so they cannot find jobs or make money. And for gangs to form, there needs to be a place where large groups of people can meet. This is usually in a defined neighborhood.

Most gangs are found in city neighborhoods.

HITTING THE HEADLINES

TROUBLE IN THE NORTHWEST

In parts of the rural northwest, gangs are a growing problem. There are drive-by shootings, graffiti, and gang rivalries. And the gangs are not just sticking to the towns but are going into public parks, including hunting areas and boat launches. One public boat launch in the Potholes Reservoir in central Washington was part of gang turf. Signs were tagged with gang graffiti. The sheriff's office reported that there were 400 gang members in a county of 85,000 people. Fish and Wildlife officer Chad McGary said, "I have three kids myself and I don't come down here unless I'm armed and I know where I'm going to be going fishing. Every single sign that we have here is tagged up. And then crossed out in red saying blue came in and tagged it up and red says 'no this is our area, not your area.'"

CHAPTER TWO

TEENS AND GANGS

Michael's friends know him as "Puppet." He joined the Two-Six gang of Chicago when he was 13 years old. The Two-Six is one of the largest street gangs in Chicago and most of its members are Latino. Michael's father was gone when he was growing up. His mom worked a lot and his friends at school were joining gangs. Michael decided to join a gang, too.

Michael's initiation was pretty brutal. Other Two-Six gang members beat him up. After they beat him up, they gave Michael a hug and welcomed him into the gang family. Michael said in an ABC News interview, "You got to take a beat down by your homies just to show them you're tough. And either you're in or you're not. That's it."

New recruits can end up bruised and bloody after their gang's initiation.

BLOOD IN, BLOOD OUT

To enter a gang, a recruit usually needs to shed some blood. This might mean the recruit is beaten up, but it might also mean the recruit has to kill someone else. Getting out of a gang may have its cost in blood, too. Gang members call this "Blood in, blood out."

HITTING THE HEADLINES

CAUGHT IN THE ACT

Some gangs make videos of their violent initiations. One video from a gang in Wisconsin went viral on Facebook. It showed a 16-year-old boy letting other gang members beat him up so that he could join the gang. The video led police straight to the gang members, who were charged with felony crimes.

Gangs may lure in recruits with their money and possessions. Recruits can see the power gang members have in neighborhoods, where they create fear in the people. And recruits can see the bonds gang members have with each other. Recruits may feel special and wanted. But then, at some point, recruits usually have to show their loyalty. This is why gangs may make recruits do special acts, called initiations, before they become official members. By going through violent initiations, recruits gain the respect of the other gang members.

Young people break into private property to impress other gang members.

13

To high school dropouts with no school, money, or family support, gangs might seem like the answer to all of their problems. Gangs can offer an identity to people who feel lost and aimless, and a feeling of power to those who have no money, job, or influence. Many vulnerable teens find the pull of gangs hard to resist.

A typical gang recruit is a young male who has dropped out of high school, and has no job and little family support. He may also have a history of problems with the law. He has lots of free time with not much to do and may feel badly about where his life is going.

AN ATTRACTIVE OPTION

There are many reasons why gangs may be attractive to the typical recruit. In dangerous neighborhoods, a gang can offer a teen protection. The members look out for each other, and it can be a way for teens to survive the tough streets where they live. Gangs may make teens feel powerful. They believe that being gang members makes others respect them.

In certain neighborhoods, teens are vulnerable to attacks on the streets if they do not belong to gangs.

BREAKING NEWS

>> Gangs also use the Internet to recruit new members, posting content that makes gang life look glamorous. They make pages on social media sites, such as Facebook and Twitter, and also post videos

Gangs may also provide a place where the teen can belong. For a teen who feels like a misfit, a gang family can become home, like "brothers and sisters." Gang members like to hang out together, have parties, and drink or take drugs. Teens may also see that their friends are joining gangs.

Gangs can become more of a family to teens than the ones they have at home.

Through their criminal activities, gangs may also move a lot of money, and teens who before were unable to find jobs can quickly make large amounts. These activities might also seem exciting to teens, giving them the thrill of breaking the law. Recruiters target teens convincing them to join—or giving them no choice but to join.

on YouTube. The Internet allows gangs to reach many more people. They may also coordinate attacks against a gang's rivals. Mostly, though, gangs use the Internet to boast about what they have done.

GANG INITIATIONS

To join a gang, recruits must be initiated. Most gangs have a distinct initiation ceremony. There are different kinds of initiations, some more violent than others. Here are examples of the most common types:

Rolled or Jumped In: This is when a recruit must fight other gang members for a certain period of time. The recruit needs to show that he or she can take the beating. Gang members want to see if the recruit is a tough person and a good fighter.

Lined In: Gang members stand in two lines and the recruit has to move down the middle of the lines while being beaten.

Sexed In: This initiation is used for female recruits to mostly male gangs. It requires them to have sex with several male gang members.

Jacked In: For their initiation, recruits must commit a crime. They might rob a house or steal a car.

Blood In: This may mean that a recruit has to be beaten. It can also mean that a recruit has to murder someone.

Fighting is a skill that most gangs value.

Courted In: In this situation a recruit is simply asked to join, without having to go through a violent initiation ceremony. The gang probably wants the talents, skills, or connections that the recruit has.

Sometimes recruits die during their gang initiations, which can be brutal and extremely violent. If they are sexed in, recruits can get diseases, such as HIV, or they may become pregnant.

Sometimes, new recruits must steal cars to prove their loyalty to a gang.

UNDERCOVER STORY
TEEN KILLED FOR GANG INITIATION

In Indiana, in March 2013, 14-year-old Depree Mims got up from the couch in his living room to get a blanket for his siblings. A loud blast rang out from the window and then Depree dropped to the ground. He had been shot in the head and he later died. The shooting was part of a gang initiation. Four men mistook Depree for a gang member, and one of them, who wanted to join the others' gang, shot at him. Depree had never been involved with gangs and was an innocent victim.

Street gangs are organized groups. They have a set of laws members must follow. There are also different roles members have within the group.

Some gang members have more violent roles than others.

GANG ROLES

New recruits start at the bottom of the gang's structure. They have the lowest status and must do the toughest jobs and carry out the orders given by gang members who are above them in the group. New members do the risky assignments and carry the gang's drugs or guns.

Higher up are the hard-core members. They have been in the gang for a while, are older, and have proven their loyalty to the gang. Hard-core members are usually the most violent.

At the top are the gang's leaders. A leader makes the final decisions for the gang. He decides what kinds of criminal activity the gang is involved with. Sometimes gang leaders direct their gangs from jail, giving their commands through phone calls or visitors.

BREAKING NEWS

>> Most violent crime comes from gangs. According to a 2011 survey by the National Gang Intelligence Center (NGIC), big cities and suburban counties see the worst gang violence. In some

Gangs may vandalize buildings and be involved in other crimes.

CRIMINAL ACTIVITY

Gangs may be involved in many types of crimes. Some might be minor, but many are serious. Members may use spray paint to tag buildings, bridges, and signs, leaving their gang's symbol or messages for other gangs. This is vandalism, which is against the law. Gangs might vandalize buildings and neighborhoods in other ways, too.

Gangs may also be involved with violent crime. They can use high-powered guns to intimidate other gangs, and they may shoot at and kill people who get in their way. Many gangs also sell drugs locally and move drugs across the country. Some gangs are involved in human trafficking, which is selling people into slavery or prostitution.

areas, gangs commit 48 percent of violent crimes. In other areas, this jumps to 90 percent. The NGIC also reports that most violent crimes come from neighborhood-based gangs and those involved with drugs.

Each gang has a unique way to identify its group. Symbols and signs tell others which gang a person belongs to. Gangs use codes to communicate, and different clothing and colors help identify gangs.

Graffiti: Made using spray paint, graffiti is a mark put on a building, sign, or structure. Not all graffiti is gang related. Some graffiti is very artistic, with some large murals showing beautiful images. Graffiti has also long been a symbol of hip-hop culture. But gang graffiti, also called tagging, is not art—it

is very different. It is used to mark territory and make people afraid. It usually shows words or symbols that may be hard to spot if you do not know much about gangs. For example, a grouping of four dots is a symbol of the Norteno gang in Sacramento, California.

Tattoos: A tattoo is another gang symbol. It shows others what gang a person is in and his or her commitment to that gang. Members may get tattoos on different parts of their bodies. Many gang tattoos go on the face, neck, chest, and hands.

HITTING THE HEADLINES

DANGEROUS HATS

In 2007, hatmaker New Era released hats with the New York Yankees logo on them. But the hats also seemed to be gang related. Some had crowns (for the Latin Kings), some were red (for the Bloods), and some were blue (for the Crips). Protesters in East Harlem, New York, demanded that the hats be removed from stores. They thought the hats would be dangerous for their neighborhood. Their protests worked, and the hats were taken out of stores that year.

Hand symbols tell others what gang a person belongs to.

These tattoos show letters that symbolize the gang, such as ESL for East Side Locos in Idaho. They can also show numbers or a picture. A five-pointed crown is a symbol for the Latin Kings. Gang tattoos can be a combination of letters, numbers, and pictures, too.

Colors and Clothing: Different colors, clothing brands, and sports logos show a person's allegiance to a gang. The Crips use the colors blue and black as their symbol, for example. Colors can be worn as hats or bandannas, while some Hispanic gangs wear a particular kind of outfit, with white T-shirts, baggy pants, and thin belts.

Hand Symbols: Most gangs use hand symbols, too. These symbols communicate what gang they belong to and show threats to another person. The symbols represent numbers, letters, or gang names.

Men run most gangs, but females can be members, too. There are also all-female gangs. These girls can be tough and violent, using guns and knives. They may get into fights with other girls and boys, too. According to the US Department of Justice, there are 60,000 to 80,000 girl gang members in the United States. In Los Angeles, California, there are around 5,000 women gangsters. Girl gangs make up 2 percent of all US gangs.

GIRL POWER

Police and members of rival gangs often overlook girls, who can usually get away with more violence than the men. Girls may be drawn to gangs for the sense of power it gives them. Many come from broken homes and find new families in gangs. Love also pulls women into gangs. They might get involved because their boyfriend is a gang member.

Female gangs can be just as tough as male gangs.

Women have different roles in gangs. Often, they hide drugs or guns when needed by the male gang members. They may deal in drugs, and even kill and use weapons. They may also have to use their bodies to get what the gang wants. Some women try to lure men from rival gangs into traps where they can be killed or beaten. Or women may pretend to like guys to spy on rival gangs.

If a woman wants to leave a gang, she may have to be beaten or kill somebody, just like the men. But pregnant women are usually allowed to leave a gang without committing any violence.

Female gang members often hide the guns and drugs of male gang members.

UNDERCOVER STORY
LOST TO GANG VIOLENCE

Tayshana Murphy was a high school basketball star and likely to be drafted into the WNBA. But her life was cut short in 2011 when gang members in the Bronx, New York, shot her. Tayshana was a member of a girl gang, and her killers were from a rival gang. There are girl gangs throughout New York, including the Harlem Hiltons, Hood Barbies, Billion Dolla Beauties, Gun Clappin Divas, and 2 Gurl Gunnas.

CHAPTER THREE

PROBLEMS WITH GANGS

Violence is all that gangs really offer members. That is something Damien learned from experience. He joined the Chicago Two Six gang when he was only 9 years old. He had been in the gang for 19 years when he was almost killed at the age of 28.

Damien was leaving a party in a rival neighborhood when someone drove up next to him. This person thought Damien was flashing gang signs, so he started shooting, hitting Damien six times—in the stomach, the thigh, and the sides. He suffered fractured bones and barely survived, and now has to use a walker to move. Damien said in a 2012 ABC News interview, "It hurts all the time."

Many gang members serve some jail time.

Damien is no stranger to violence and crime. In his years in the gang he had been arrested more than 50 times and charged with assault with weapons and possession of a firearm. He said, "If you ain't got no job, you ain't got nowhere to go. After that, well, you're going to turn to the streets. The streets is calling you."

UNDERCOVER STORY

GANG HOMICIDES

According to the 2011 National Youth Gang Survey, most gang homicides occur in large cities. In Chicago and Los Angeles, gangs cause nearly half of all homicides. These two cities are considered to be the gang capitals of the United States.

A VIOLENT LIFE

Gangs are involved in some of the most dangerous aspects of society. Guns may be the tools they need to survive, and drugs may be how they make their money. And death and violence may be how they keep their power. It can be a lifestyle of battles and wars that no one wins. This affects gang members, their families, and their communities.

Guns and other weapons are used by many gang members.

For a gang member, a gun may be a source of power. It can make others fearful. In gangs, guns command respect. They give members the ability to commit crimes, threaten others, and protect themselves against other gangs who have guns. With their guns, gang members may commit many different crimes and participate in gang wars and shootouts.

GANG CRIME

The National Youth Gang Survey reports on gang-related crimes in the United States. In 2011, property crime, which involves stealing or vandalizing property such as a car or a house, increased just over 51 percent from the previous year.

Guns make gangs more powerful on the streets.

BREAKING NEWS

>> Social media are becoming a tool to start violence between gangs. Different gangs taunt each other through posts on Facebook and YouTube, which leads to violence on the streets. But what

Violent crimes, such as murder and shootings, had the second biggest increase of 48 percent. And drug sales increased by almost 33 percent.

The survey also found that certain factors influence gang violence.

Gangs often steal cars, use them for criminal activity, and then burn the cars to destroy the evidence.

In 2011, issues with drugs caused the most violence. The second-highest factor was problems between gangs. The third-highest factor was issues related to gang members returning from jail. Crime keeps most gangs operating. It helps them run their business of selling and moving drugs.

gangs do not realize is that these same posts can be used as evidence to put members in jail. The New York City Police Department used posts and text messages to arrest several gang members in 2013.

One of the main factors that draw people to gangs is the promise of money. For teens growing up in poverty, gangs may give them all the money they need. But that money is dirty—it usually comes from selling drugs and other illegal activities.

Many gangs make their money by selling drugs.

Selling Drugs: Street, prison, and outlaw motorcycle gangs are the main sellers of drugs in the United States. They may also smuggle drugs into the country and produce and move drugs from state to state. Many drugs sold are hard drugs, such as crack cocaine and heroin, although gangs also sell marijuana.

BREAKING NEWS

>> El Paso, Texas, is full of gangs. Just across the border is the town of Juarez in Mexico. It is the base for smuggling drugs from Mexico to the United

Big Business: Gangs can make millions of dollars each month from selling drugs, illegally selling guns, selling stolen goods, and prostitution. To hide all their money, gangs may own businesses, such as barbershops and music stores. The gangs can funnel their money through the businesses. The illegal cash then looks like earnings from those businesses.

Drugs in Communities: By being the main drug suppliers, many gangs feed drug addictions in communities across the United States. Being addicted to drugs can destroy a person's life. Most addicts eventually lose everything—from a family's support to a job and a home.

Drug addiction can ruin many people's lives.

States. Gang members drive drugs over the border, or drugs are strapped onto the bodies of people who then walk across the border. Some gangs ship drugs internationally, to and from Europe and Asia.

Being involved with a gang can be incredibly dangerous. Members may have a high risk of death, arrest, and serving jail time. Many gang members die young or waste their youth in jail cells. It is a lifestyle that can lead to a dismal future.

A gang member's home can be a target for the bullets of rival gangs.

DEATH, INJURY, AND CRIME

Gang members are often shot at and killed by other members. Their homes may also become shooting targets. This means that a gang member's family also has a risk of being injured or murdered. Many gang members are arrested numerous times and charged with serious offenses, which gives them criminal records.

BREAKING NEWS

>> In a 2009 report in the *Journal of School Health*, it was stated that drug and alcohol use was more common in schoolkids who belonged to gangs than it was for non-gang members. Here are the results of that study:

EDUCATION AND EMPLOYMENT

Most gang recruits are high school dropouts. They may stop their education early and have difficulty reading and writing. Before joining a gang, these recruits may also have had problems getting a job. If they want to leave a gang, members have to be prepared to struggle. Without a high school diploma, finding jobs outside of gang life is not easy, and having a criminal record can create barriers to employment.

EARLY PREGNANCY

For female gang members, early pregnancy may be a risk they take for being involved in a gang. They may become pregnant from being sexed-in to the gang. Or they may want to get pregnant at a young age as their only way out of a gang.

Female gang members may become pregnant after their initiation.

- Binge drinking: 43 percent of members and 24 percent of non-gang members
- Marijuana use: 54 percent of members and 26 percent of non-gang members
- Drug selling: 51 percent of members and 9 percent of non-gang members

gang family could give things. She was a hothead. She stole cars and sold drugs. She was angry and had no idea how to deal with her anger.

Jessica then experienced a lot of pain while in the gang. She found out that gang life had no love to offer her. "Only things the streets got to offer is money, death or [jail time]—because they [gang members] don't want to end up in jail, so they going to give you the gun and tell you to go out and shoot somebody," she said in a 2011 ABC News interview.

Selling drugs is a quick way to make money in gangs.

So Jessica decided to get out of the Black Disciples. She wanted to turn her life around. In 2011, she was attending community college to study criminal justice. And she found a new way to deal with her anger. "When I get angry from now on, I just write," Jessica said. "I use this stuff that goes on around me and turn it into stories and maybe I'm going to write a book someday. I think I could be a motivation to stop all this violence and stuff."

A NEW LIFE

Getting out of a gang may not easy, but it can be done. And there is hope for ex-gang members.

With education or job training, many can find jobs. They can learn how to live their lives without the influence of gangs.

Without a high school education, there are few options for teens to become independent adults.

UNDERCOVER STORY

EX-GANG MEMBERS HELPING OTHERS

Gang-prevention programs keep kids from joining gangs. The Boys & Girls Clubs of America has around 500 anti-gang programs, and they are using ex-gang members to help run the programs. One of those ex-gang members is Jackie Ybarra. She spent much of her teen years in gangs but quit after attending a Boys & Girls Club program. It helped her graduate from high school. The program also provided Ybarra with a mentor who understood what she was going through. Many mentors in the programs are ex-gang members, too.

Most parents do not want their kids to be in gangs. Sometimes they just cannot see the signs, though. And by the time they realize their kid is in a gang, it may be too late. Their teen may already be a member and part of a gang family. That is why it is important for parents, friends, and teachers to know what signs to look for in teens. If those signs are caught early enough, a teen can be stopped from joining a gang. Here are some of the early signs that a teen is becoming involved with a gang:

New Friends: A teen suddenly has new friends. These friends may seem rougher or tougher than the teen's old friends.

Gang Symbols: The teen has gang symbols written on his or her books, clothing, or locker. The teen might also start wearing a bandanna or hat in a certain color. Watch for tattoos or hand signals, too.

No Interest: A teen might start skipping school or not caring about homework. The teen stops listening to his or her parents, too.

Bandannas can be a gang sign.

UNDERCOVER STORY

GANGS IN SCHOOLS

It is common to find gangs and drugs in schools. In a 2010 survey by the National Center on Addiction and Substance Abuse at Columbia University (CASA), nearly one-third of kids between the ages of 12 and 17 said their schools had gang and drug problems. In fact, public schools are where gangs find most of their recruits.

Using Drugs and Alcohol: The teen starts partying at night and on the weekends. A parent or friend then sees signs of drug and alcohol use by the teen. The teen sleeps late, has mood swings, or may have drug tools, such as a drug pipe or syringes, in his or her room.

Partying late at night can be a warning sign of a teen's changing lifestyle.

Weapons and Cash: A teen who has large amounts of cash is probably involved in something that is illegal. And weapons, such as guns or knives, are a red flag that a teen is involved with a gang.

Getting Arrested: Finally, if a teen is arrested, it is important to understand what the charges are. An arrest confirms that a teen is doing something illegal.

Getting out of a gang is not easy. If someone chooses to leave, it can be a slow and painful process. And sometimes gangs do not let members leave alive.

WHY LEAVE?

After a while, the pull of gang life weakens for some people. Members may start to mature and grow out of the gang lifestyle.

Some begin to have families and care for their partners and children. They may want to provide a good life for them, and do not want the gang violence to reach their homes. They also may have a job and need to focus on the job's responsibilities.

Children protested against gang violence at an anti-gang march in Los Angeles, California, in 2012.

BREAKING NEWS

>> A gang tattoo is a constant reminder of a past an ex-gang member wants to forget. It can tell others of a person's gang history and can be

A gang member may have had one too many bad experiences in the gang. It can push that person away. Maybe a close friend was killed. Maybe the violence becomes too hard to take after a while. Or the police might be pressuring the member to leave the gang.

Tattoos remain a permanent reminder of a person's past gang involvement.

GETTING OUT

Whatever the reason, getting out may require the member to become involved in some violent act. This could be murder or it could mean letting other gang members beat the person up. Sometimes gang members can just leave without any violence. Intervention programs can help members leave gangs, and also provide services that help ex-gang members get back on their feet.

intimidating. Tattoos can also prevent ex-gang members from getting jobs. Some intervention programs offer tattoo removal as a service, and this can help ex-gang members start afresh in their new lives.

CHAPTER FIVE

SOCIETY AND GANGS

Gangs and gang violence may have serious costs to society. Some may be financial, and some may cause problems for the justice and penal systems. Then there is the worst cost of all—the lives taken by gang violence.

DRIVE-BY SHOOTINGS

When someone drives up in a car and shoots at a person, another car, or a building, that is a drive-by shooting. The shooter or shooters then quickly leave the crime scene in the car, which makes it difficult to identify them.

Gang members usually hit someone from another gang in the shootings. But often innocent people are hurt or killed as they are caught in the crossfire. Sometimes these people are not even on the street—they are inside their homes when the bullets hit them.

Innocent people can be killed from the stray bullets of gang shootings.

In areas where drive-by shootings occur, community members may start to feel afraid in their own neighborhoods. Some choose not to leave their houses at night. But even inside their houses they can be unsafe. Across the United States, news reports tell of innocent children and adults killed by stray bullets from gang members' guns.

Neighborhoods become unsafe for everyone living in areas with gangs.

HITTING THE HEADLINES
INNOCENT DEATHS

It seems that every month innocent children die from drive-by shootings or stray bullets. That is what happened to 11-year-old Taylani Mazyck. In June 2013, she was walking with her mom in her Bronx neighborhood. Someone shot at a gang member, but the bullet hit Taylani in the neck instead. It lodged in her spine and doctors immediately feared that she might be paralyzed.

Prisons in the United States are filled with gang members. Some form gangs inside the prison's walls, while many belong to gangs in the outside world. There are high costs to keep these criminals in jail, and the people of the United States pay those costs.

PRISON POPULATION

The US prison population is big. It tops 2.2 million people, which makes it the highest in the world. Even China, the country with the most people in the world, does not have as many people in jail. A high proportion of that population are gang members, and with gangs working inside prisons, members are not being changed by jail time. They just continue their gangster lifestyle while doing their time.

It costs US taxpayers around $60 million each year to keep those 2.2 million people in jail. And the jails are not even succeeding in helping prisoners change their ways. Violence is a serious problem inside jails.

US jails are filled with many gang members.

UNDERCOVER STORY

A DANGEROUS PRISON GANG

The Barrio Azteca is one the most violent prison gangs in the United States. Many of its 2,000 members are inside Texas prisons, but they also live in communities in Texas and New Mexico. This gang is heavily involved with drug selling and smuggling, and is linked to the Mexican drug cartels, a network of criminals involved in selling and exporting illegal drugs.

Around 60 percent of those who are released end up back in jail. Many states have tough sentencing laws for gang violence, which can result in sentences that are 15 years or longer. While these sentences keep gang members off the streets, they also increase the jail costs that citizens must pay.

Jail does not prevent inmates from committing crimes when released.

To keep kids out of gangs, prevention and education may be the keys. Programs that keep kids off the streets after school are important in areas with high gang involvement. They can provide the support missing in the homes of kids vulnerable to gangs, and also simply give kids something to do with their free time. A youth program can be the support group that teens search for in gang families.

Anti-gang education is also important, for both teens and their parents. If parents know the signs of gang involvement, they can step in and stop teens from being in gangs. And knowing the real consequences of gang involvement, such as death or jail time, may be what teens need to avoid joining.

Youth groups help keep at-risk teens off dangerous streets.

BREAKING NEWS

>> One after-school program in New York City helps teens produce films. It is called the Teen Producers Academy, at the Maysles Institute. Fourteen of the teens involved made a film about teen gun violence

Being involved with sports can be a positive way to avoid gang life.

Safe and Sound: Located in Milwaukee, Wisconsin, the Safe & Sound program has locations in 19 neighborhoods, where teens can go after school. These are positive places where kids can feel safe from the crime and drugs on the street. The program encourages teens to set goals, and then provides activities that help them fulfill those goals. The program also encourages teens to educate others about the dangers of being involved with gangs.

Boys & Girls Clubs of America: These national clubs have many youth programs, some of which are targeted toward youth at risk of joining gangs, particularly those aged 6–18. Many of these programs have ex-gang members as mentors. They help teens graduate from high school, provide assistance with homework, and keep teens busy after school.

PROGRAMS THAT HELP

There are many groups around the United States that run youth programs to help kids stay out of gangs.

in Harlem, called *Triggering Wounds: A Story of Guns and Violence in Harlem*. The film premiered at the 2013 Tribeca Film Festival and was nominated for Best Documentary in a youth category.

GANGS—THE TRUTH

The truth about gangs is that they are found across the United States and bring violence and drugs to the streets. Gangs may be attractive to vulnerable teens living in socially disadvantaged areas. In these places, teens may have little adult supervision and lots of free time. Many drop out of school and cannot find jobs. They may also be threatened by the violence in their neighborhoods.

Gangs can provide protection, money, purpose, and a family for these teens. But what gangs offer is balanced by the violence and crime they can bring to communities. Gun violence is common in gangs, and many gang members end up injured, dead, or in jail. This violence breaks up communities and kills many innocent people as well as gang members.

Teens who stay connected with their families have a better chance of resisting the lure of gangs and crime.

UNDERCOVER STORY

HELPING A TEEN ESCAPE

To gang and drug counselor Carlos Rodriguez, helping teens get away from gangs is his life. Rodriguez works for Omni Youth Services in a suburb of Chicago, one of the most gang-filled cities in the United States. More and more gangs are moving out from the city to the suburbs, and it was here that Rodriguez helped Ivan Ibarra escape a gang. Rodriguez counseled Ibarra, called him often, and met him for lunches. "I found it weird," Ibarra said. "This guy was calling me and sitting down with me. We'd have interesting conversations about life, family, and culture." But the tactics worked and, after four years of working with Rodriguez, Ibarra left the gang.

HOPE FOR THE FUTURE

There is hope, though, for those who want to escape the pull of gangs. After-school programs keep teens occupied and provide the support they need to stay in school and graduate. They can also provide support to teens who are vulnerable to becoming gang members and help them understand the consequences of gang life. Parents and teachers, too, can learn the warning signs of gang involvement so they can intervene with at-risk teens. Getting teens off the streets is vital. It keeps them away from the crime and violence of gangs.

GLOSSARY

assassin The murderer of an important person.

brutal Very violent.

burglarize To illegally enter a building in order to commit a crime.

detention Being kept in an area by a police officer.

felony A serious crime, usually involving violence.

graffiti Writing or drawing on a surface in a public place.

homie The slang name for a member of a peer group.

hybrid Something made by combining two different elements.

initiation Something people are asked to do before being allowed to join a gang.

intimidate To frighten someone in order to make them do what you want them to do.

juvenile Relating to young people.

loyalty Strong feeling of support for someone else or a group of people.

overwhelmed Having feelings that are too strong to take.

poverty Being very poor.

prevention Stopping something from happening.

prostitution Engaging in sexual activities for money.

recruit To enlist new members to a group; also, a new member.

rival A group that competes for control of something.

supervision Observing and directing someone.

tattoo A permanent mark made on a person's body by putting ink into a person's skin.

territory An area of land that is controlled by a person or group.

vulnerable Open to attack or harm.

FOR MORE INFORMATION

BOOKS

Bow, James. *Gangs*. New York, NY: Crabtree Publishing, 2012.

Hile, Lori. *Gangs*. Chicago, IL: Heinemann, 2013.

Lane, Brian, and Laura Buller. *Crime & Detection*. New York, NY: DK Publishing, 2005.

ORGANIZATIONS

Gang Rescue and Support Project
701 South Logan Street
Suite 109
Denver, CO 80209
(303) 777-3117
Web site: http://www.graspyouth.org
This program works to prevent teens from joining gangs and also helps them get out of gangs.

Teen Line
P.O. Box 48750
Los Angeles, CA 90048
(310) 855-HOPE (4673) or (800) TLC-TEEN (352-8336)
Web site: http://teenlineonline.org
A site and phone line run for teens by teens that deals with a variety of issues that affect young people.

WEB SITES

Due to the changing nature of Internet links, Rosen Publishing has developed an online list of Web sites related to the subject of this book. This site is updated regularly. Please use this link to access the list:

http://www.rosenlinks.com/UCS/Gang

INDEX